S0-ABU-034

A Long Winter Nap

SRA

Columbus, OH

Front Cover © Kenneth M. Highfill / Photo Researchers, Inc.; **3** ©
Jeffrey Lepore / Photo Researchers, Inc.; **4-5** © Cordelia Molloy
/ Photo Researchers, Inc.; **6-7** © Thomas & Pat Leeson / Photo
Researchers, Inc.; **8-9** © Peter Arnold, Inc. / Alamy; **10** © Kenneth M.
Highfill / Photo Researchers, Inc.; **11** © Annie Griffiths Belt / CORBIS;
12-13 © Royalty-Free / Corbis; **14-15** © Arco Images / Alamy; **Back
Cover** © Kenneth M. Highfill / Photo Researchers, Inc.

SRAonline.com

 SRA

Copyright © 2008 by SRA/McGraw-Hill.

All rights reserved. No part of this publication may be
reproduced or distributed in any form or by any means,
or stored in a database or retrieval system, without the
prior written consent of The McGraw-Hill Companies,
Inc., including, but not limited to, network storage or
transmission, or broadcast for distance learning.
An Open Court Curriculum.

Printed in China.

Send all inquiries to this address:
SRA/McGraw-Hill
4400 Easton Commons
Columbus, OH 43219

ISBN: 978-0-07-608739-6
MHID: 0-07-608739-5

1 2 3 4 5 6 7 8 9 NOR 13 12 11 10 09 08 07

The McGraw·Hill Companies

Black bear eating berries

Saving Energy

All animals need energy to live. They need energy to breathe, move, and digest food. Animals, like people, get energy from the foods they eat. Bears get their energy from a diet of berries and fish. Squirrels get energy from grains, seeds, and nuts.

How does energy get into these foods? First, a plant absorbs sunlight through its leaves. The plant uses energy from the sun to make glucose, which is a type of sugar. Some of this sugar is stored in the plant.

An animal eats the plant. Its body absorbs this stored glucose. The body then converts it into the energy it needs to move, eat, and breathe. Some of this energy is also stored to be used later.

This is similar to the way a car engine works. Fuel is put into a car. The engine converts the fuel into energy to make the car run. The fuel that is not used remains in the gas tank to be used later.

Eating for energy is easy when there is lots of food around. But cold weather makes it hard for animals to find food. Many plants they eat do not grow in winter. Animals must then use the fat they stored in their bodies in the fall. If they run out of this "food" they will not live.

An animal's body also uses more energy in cold weather. When it is cold outside it takes more energy to stay warm than it does at other times of the year.

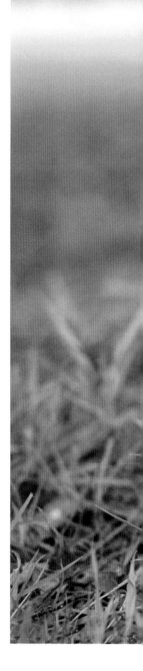

Squirrel eating a nut

A Special Kind of Sleep

Some animals hibernate to live through the winter. When they do this, the animals go into a special kind of deep sleep. They live mostly off the food stored in their bodies. While they are hibernating their bodies use less energy. If the animals use less energy they need less food.

Hibernation might sound simple, but it is more than just a winter nap. Scientists have studied what really happens to animals that hibernate.

As the weather grows cold, hibernating animals get ready for the long months ahead. They eat more food than usual to store up a thick layer of fat. As they sleep, they will use this fat for energy. They also put on a layer of special fat called "brown fat" near their heart, liver, and brain.

Some hibernating animals also store food. They hide nuts, seeds, and berries in their burrows and dens. In these cozy spots the animals are protected from severe cold and hungry predators.

Squirrel stocking up on acorns before winter

When an animal hibernates its body changes. Normal body temperature for most mammals is around 99F. When they hibernate it falls below 50°F. Most animals breathe many times per minute. Their hearts beat quickly too. But when they hibernate everything slows down.

A woodchuck's heart beats seventy-five times per minute when it is awake. When it hibernates its heart beats only about four times per minute. An arctic ground squirrel may take as few as two breaths per minute when hibernating!

Black bear mother and cubs coming out of den

Who Hibernates, and How?

Most people think that bears hibernate in the winter. According to scientists, this is not true. Bears just sleep longer during cold weather. They do not really hibernate. Scientists know this because a bear's body temperature does not drop in winter. On warmer winter days, bears get up, move around, and find food.

They protect themselves from the cold by living in dens. Some dens are in caves. Others are in hollow tree stumps or in holes at the bases of large trees.

Ground squirrels and woodchucks are animals that do truly hibernate. During the winter, arctic ground squirrels curl up to sleep in underground nests. Their body temperatures drop almost to the freezing point— 32°F. During this time, they can lose up to half their body weight. They wake up only once or twice a month to eat from the food they've stored in their nests. They hibernate for seven or eight months. That's over half of the year!

You may know when it's time to go to sleep because you have a set bedtime or you feel sleepy.

Scientists think that several events start hibernation in animals. One event is colder temperatures. Another is shorter days and longer nights. As winter approaches there are fewer hours of daylight. When days are shorter there is less time to find food. When nights are longer, animals that sleep when it is dark have more time to do so.

The change in seasons triggers hibernation.

When one or more of these events happen, a natural chemical enters the animal's blood. This is called *hibernation induction trigger*, or HIT.

HIT slows the heart rate and other body functions. It also protects important cells. This way, organs such as the heart and brain remain safe during the winter.

Scientists are still learning about HIT. Some scientists have taken blood with HIT in it from hibernating squirrels. They injected this blood into active squirrels. The active squirrels began to hibernate!

Awake and Alive

How do you wake up in time for school each morning? Maybe an alarm clock goes off. Maybe a parent wakes you. But have you ever woken up just because you were not sleepy anymore or because you were hungry? When that happens your body is telling you what to do, just like an alarm clock.

Animals' bodies act as alarm clocks too. Hibernating animals simply wake up when the weather gets warmer so their bodies can get the food they need.

Arctic ground squirrels

The first thing an animal's body does to wake up from hibernation is raise its temperature. To do this it may shiver to create heat. The brown fat stored near the animal's organs is turned into heat. This warms the important organs quickly.

It takes a while for animals to get back to normal. When they first wake up they are weak and slow. This is because they have lost most of their body fat. It is easier for predators to catch animals when they are slow.

When you first wake up in the morning you are probably groggy. Then you slowly become alert. Animals waking after hibernation are the same. After a while they are fully awake. They return to their regular sleep habit. They also return to their regular diet. In only a few days they reach a normal body weight.

After the long winter months they are able to find plenty of food again. They lived through a cold winter with very little food by sleeping to save energy!

Vocabulary

diet (dī´ it) (page 3) *n.* The food and drink eaten by an animal.

absorbs (əb sorbz´) (page 3) *v.* Takes in.

converts (kən vûrts´) (page 4) A form of the verb **convert**: To change something into something different.

layer (lā´ ər) (page 6) *n.* One thickness of something.

predators (pre´ də tərz) (page 6) *n.* Plural form of **predator**: An animal that hunts and kills other animals for food.

alert (ə lûrt´) (page 15) *adj.* Awake and prepared to act.

Comprehension Focus: Summarizing

1. Reread page four. Summarize how cold winter weather affects some animals

2. Reread page eight. Summarize how an animal's body changes when it hibernates.